ABOUT
EVERYDAY LIFE

GROLIER
BOOKS

PUBLISHER	Joseph R. DeVarennes	
PUBLICATION DIRECTOR	Kenneth H. Pearson	
ADVISORS	Roger Aubin	
	Robert Furlonger	
EDITORIAL SUPERVISOR	Jocelyn Smyth	
PRODUCTION MANAGER	Ernest Homewood	
PRODUCTION ASSISTANTS	Martine Gingras	Kathy Kishimoto
	Catherine Gordon	Peter Thomlison
CONTRIBUTORS	Alison Dickie	Nancy Prasad
	Bill Ivy	Lois Rock
	Jacqueline Kendel	Merebeth Switzer
	Anne Langdon	Dave Taylor
	Sheila Macdonald	Alison Tharen
	Susan Marshall	Donna Thomson
	Pamela Martin	Pam Young
	Colin McCance	
SENIOR EDITOR	Robin Rivers	
EDITORS	Brian Cross	Ann Martin
	Anne Louise Mahoney	Mayta Tannenbaum
PUBLICATION ADMINISTRATOR	Anna Good	
ART AND DESIGN	Richard Comely	Ronald Migliore
	Robert B. Curry	Penelope Moir
	George Elliott	Marion Stuck
	Marilyn James	Bill Suddick
	Robert Johanssen	Sue Wilkinson

Canadian Cataloguing in Publication Data

Main entry under title:

Questions kids ask about everyday life.

(Questions kids ask ; 15)
ISBN 0-7172-2554-2

1. Science—Miscellanea—Juvenile literature.
2. Children's questions and answers.
I. Smyth, Jocelyn.   II. Comely, Richard.   III. Series.

Q163.Q46 1988   j500   C89-093165-8

Questions Kids Ask . . . about EVERYDAY LIFE

continued

What is a shadow?

To understand what a shadow is, you must first know what light is.

Light is a form of energy which can come from natural sources (the sun and stars) or from artificial sources (candles, lamps and lasers). Light travels in waves, but unlike sound, which also travels in waves, light can't go through walls or around corners. That is why you might not be able to see your neighbor's dog even if you can hear it barking. Light waves cannot bend by themselves, so any object that blocks their path will create a darkened area, or shadow, on the side away from the source of light.

When were bathtubs first used?

There were bathtubs with hot and cold running water on the Greek island of Crete 4000 years ago. Later, the Romans were famous for their huge baths, some of which could hold 1500 people. Such public baths were popular in several countries until people started worrying about getting diseases from the water.

In the Dark Ages, few people thought it necessary or even healthy to bathe. After the late 1600s, however, people started using portable tubs which they filled and emptied by hand.

There were no bathtubs with attached plumbing in Buckingham Palace when Queen Victoria came to the throne in 1837, and none in the White House until 1851. A survey in the 1880s showed that five out of six people in American cities had no bathtub.

It wasn't until after World War I that the age of modern plumbing finally began and people gradually started installing bathtubs in their homes.

What were the first mirrors made of?

Today we take glass mirrors for granted, but you may be surprised to learn that there was no such thing until the 1300s. And for 300 years after that, there were none that produced an undistorted reflection.

Human beings' first mirror was probably the still water of a clear pool. Then, in the Bronze Age, about 5500 years ago, the Sumerians discovered that polished metals made a good reflecting surface to see themselves in. They set their bronze mirrors in plain handles of wood, ivory and gold.

The ancient Greeks formed the first known school for mirror making. Students learned the delicate art of sand polishing a metal without scratching it.

Why do we have leap years?

A leap year is one in which February has 29 days instead of the usual 28.

   We have leap years because of the way our calendar works. The length of the calendar year is 365 days, but the solar year—the time it takes the earth to go around the sun—is actually 365.24 days long. The calendar makes up for the extra one-quarter day each year by adding a day every four years. Leap years occur in years that are exactly divisible by 4, like 1740 and 1988. Years ending in 00 must be divisible by 400 to be leap years—2000 will be a leap year but 1900 was not.

   If people who were born on February 29 only celebrated their birthday every four years they wouldn't have many birthday parties, so they usually celebrate on February 28.

Who wrote "Happy Birthday to You"?

The melody of "Happy Birthday to You" was first published in 1893. It was written by two sisters, Mildred and Patty Hill from Louisville, Kentucky. Mildred was a church organist and composer. Patty was a school principal.

The song was originally called "Good Morning To All." No one knows who changed the words but whoever it was probably didn't know that the song would become the most frequently sung song in the world!

DID YOU KNOW . . . every day at least 10 million people celebrate their birthday!

Why do we polish our shoes?

People often judge others by the state of their shoes. If your shoes are scuffed and dirty, people might think you are too. Polished shoes seem to earn respect.

But there's another very practical reason for polishing shoes—especially if they're made of leather. Leather needs to be cleaned and oiled so it doesn't dry out. Shoe polish, which is made of oils, helps your shoes last a long time. So if you own a pair of shoes you really don't like . . . don't polish them and they'll wear out sooner.

DID YOU KNOW . . . travelers say that going through customs is much easier if their shoes are clean and well-cared for.

Why do people wear neckties?

Neckties aren't very comfortable and they don't seem to serve any practical purpose. Nonetheless people wear them . . . because they are fashionable.

The first recorded neckwear did have a practical purpose. In the first century B.C., Roman soldiers soaked lengths of cloth in water and wrapped them around their neck to cool themselves down in the heat of the day.

The modern necktie goes back to another military custom. In 1668, soldiers from Croatia came to France wearing linen and muslin scarves around their necks. Fashion-conscious French men and women liked the idea and began wearing linen or lace neckwear, knotted in the center, with long flaring ends. They called the ties *cravates,* after the Croatians.

The fashion spread and soon one of the hottest topics of discussion in European capitals was the proper way to tie the new neckwear. Since that time, neckwear—long or short, wide or narrow—has been the fashion for men and sometimes for women.

11

How did coins get their names?

The word *coin* comes from a Latin word meaning "wedge"—and, in fact, the earliest coins were wedge-shaped, like a piece of pie.

The quarter got its name from an early Spanish silver dollar called a piece of eight. To make change people chopped this coin into eight pie-shaped bits. Two of these bits equalled a quarter of a dollar. People still sometimes call a quarter "two bits."

The dollar gets its name from a German coin known as a *taler*. In the 17th century a German emperor of Spain used this coin in his new country. Spanish explorers took it with them to the Americas where it soon became known as a dollar.

The word *dime,* which is ten cents or one-tenth of a dollar, comes from an Old French word meaning "a tenth." The popular name for our five-cent piece comes from the metal from which the original coin was made—nickel. Similarly, our one-cent pieces are sometimes called "coppers" because they used to be made of copper. Their more common name, penny, comes from Old

English *penig*. And that is thought to have come from a Latin word for cloth, because cloth used to be exchanged for other goods in parts of Europe.

DID YOU KNOW . . . Canada didn't get its own mint until 1900. Because there was a shortage of coins, people in Prince Edward Island punched holes in Spanish silver coins and called them "holey dollars."

Why were umbrellas invented?

Would you believe that umbrellas were invented in a desert land where it hardly ever rained? It's true.

The umbrella originated in Mesopotamia around 1400 B.C. It was made from palm leaves, feathers and stretched papyrus (a reed-like plant and its purpose was to protect people from the harsh sun. (That explains the name, which comes from the Latin, meaning "little shade.")

Originally umbrellas were rare and a sign of rank and distinction. In early Egypt, they reminded people of the goddess Nut, whose body, they believed, formed the sky. So umbrellas were held only over the heads of the nobility. It was a great honor to be invited to stand under the royal umbrella since the shade represented the queen's or king's protection.

DID YOU KNOW . . . in ancient Greece and Rome, only women used umbrella sunshades. Men considered it unmanly, and were ridiculed if caught using one.

Where does tap water come from?

If you could see through the walls and floors of your home, you'd see an amazing network of pipes that make up the plumbing system. Not only does it bring you clean water, it also takes the used, dirty water away. But where does the water come from and how does it get to you?

Most towns and cities are located near lakes and rivers because the people who first settled there needed a constant source of water to survive. Sometimes lakes and rivers dry up, and certain towns and cities are far from fresh water, so people must have another source of water. Extra water, stored in huge containers called reservoirs, is used in place of water from natural sources. People who live far from natural water sources drill wells and pump water from the ground.

15

Why are stop signs painted red?

Do you want to stand out in a crowd? Wear something red. It's a highly visible color. You can't miss anything red because red objects appear closer than they actually are. Red has the longest wave length of all the colors. This means you can see it from a long distance. Red is also a warm, stimulating color. In the early days, when primitive people saw red, it was usually fire—and that could mean danger! So it makes sense that we paint our stop signs red. They stand out on the street, they stimulate us to be alert and they make us think danger!

Who invented windshield wipers?

In 1902, Mary Anderson from Birmingham, Alabama, was visiting New York City. While she was there it rained nearly every day. Whenever she rode the electric trolley cars through the city, she was terrified. The drivers couldn't see out their windshields and had to keep stopping to rub moist tobacco or onions on their windshields to coat them with oil. As you can imagine, it didn't work very well. The traffic jams were terrible.

When Mary got home, she got a wooden handle and put a rubber blade on the end. Drivers had to move this wiper over the windshield by hand, but those who tried her new window cleaning device thought it was wonderful. Car manufacturers eventually realized that windshield wipers were essential, and figured out how to make them work automatically.

How did dogs get their names?

Dogs have names like Lassie or Rover. But each type of dog has a name, too. Have you ever wondered how your dog got its name?

A long time ago, humans tamed wild dogs which were probably wolf cubs or jackals. Soon people realized that tame

dogs could be bred to do different jobs. Dogs with long noses were bred to track the scent of birds and small prey. Dogs that smelled the air and pointed or set their bodies to guide hunters were called pointers and setters. Dogs that brought back dead birds and game were called retrievers. Dogs that went down holes in the ground after small animals were called terriers, after the Latin word *terra* meaning "earth."

Many dogs were named after the place they were bred, such as Newfoundlands, Labradors,

Afghans and Alsatians. Chihuahuas were first bred in Mexico, Pekingese in China, and Dalmatians in Dalmatia, Yugoslavia. Saint Bernards were bred by the monks of Saint Bernard to help travelers in the snowy mountains. Spaniel comes from the Old French word *espaignol* which means Spanish.

The Dobermans get their name from Louis Doberman, a 19th-century German tax collector who bred local dogs to protect him when he carried money. In fact, the Germans bred and named many dogs. Dachshund means "badger dog" in German, and the poodle gets its name from the German word *pudel* meaning "to splash in the water."

There are over 400 modern breeds of dogs. If you want to find out where your dog got its name, a good dictionary can usually tell you.

Why did they ever start making shoes with high heels?

When you think of high heels you think of women's shoes. But the first high heeled shoes were worn in 16th-century France by men!

They began by adding slightly raised heels to riding boots to hold the foot in the stirrup. Then, during the Middle Ages, streets were full of garbage and waste, and boots with elevated heels were very practical.

In the 1600s, the fad for real high heels was started by a very short man—King Louis XIV of France. Louis was so conscious of his height, he had inches added to the heels of his shoes. The men and women at court wanted to be like their king and ordered bootmakers to heighten their heels too. This forced King Louis to get even higher heels!

The fashion spread from France to the rest of Europe and eventually to America. In time, the heels of men's shoes got lower, but the heels of women's shoes climbed higher and grew narrower. By the 1920s "high heels" referred only to women's footwear.

Why do stairs and floors sometimes creak?

Even if you don't have a ghost in your house, there's a simple explanation for creaking stairs and floors.

Creaky stairs are very common. Just think how many times people go up and down them. They have to be well made to stand all that strain. The part of the stair you walk on is called a tread, and it is supported by pieces of wood called risers. After a while, a tread may pull loose from the risers and rub against them. The next thing you know, the stairs start groaning under every footstep.

Floors are supported by large wooden beams, or joists. On top of these joists is a sub-floor, which is usually made of plywood, and on top of that are the floor boards. If the floor boards or the sub-floor are too wet or too dry, they become warped or crooked. As well, the boards and the nails in them may start working loose as they get older. And when a floor board is loose, it rubs against the edges of the next board, causing squeaks and creaks.

Click!

Creak!

How many toothpicks can you get from a cord of wood?

First of all, you need to know how big a cord is. A cord of wood is a pile that is 1.25 metres (4 feet) high, 1.25 metres (4 feet) wide and 2.5 metres (8 feet) long. That sounds like a lot of toothpicks, doesn't it? It is! In fact, you can get 7 500 000 toothpicks from a cord of wood.

How big is dust?

We all know that dust specks are very small, but you may be surprised to find out just *how* very small they are. A speck of true dust is smaller than 1/1000 of a millimetre (1/25 000 of an inch). Coarser dust particles can be about five times that size.

Most ordinary dust in the air is made of fine particles of mineral matter. It comes from dry earth or crumbling rock and is carried through the air by wind currents.

The smallest dust may be picked up by the wind over and over again. Because of its size and weight, coarser dust tends to settle on the ground.

Volcanic dust is made of small particles of ash less than 1/16 of a millimetre (1/500 of an inch). It is released into the air after a volcanic explosion and can travel great distances.

Who decides what is good manners?

There are thousands of different cultures on this planet, and each has its own customs and ways of showing respect. But there is one simple rule of good manners that applies to everyone: treat other people the way you would like to be treated.

In the 20th century there aren't nearly as many rules to learn as there were even 100 years ago. As the world changes so do manners. Would you believe that a 16th-century book on manners advised the reader who could not swallow a piece of food to "turn round discreetly and throw it somewhere." What would your mom and dad say if you were to follow this advice? In 2500 B.C., the Egyptians wrote the first known book describing good manners. The ancient Greeks and Romans also had strict rules. During the Middle Ages in Europe, the Code of Chivalry was the set of rules for boys who wanted to be knights. Chivalry became the basis of good manners in later centuries.

Some cultures and religions still have very strict rules of behavior. Many Jewish people still obey the rules in the Talmud which describe how and what to eat. Arabs eat only with their right hand because they believe that the left hand is unclean. The Japanese never put food on top of their rice whereas the Chinese always do. If you enter a Japanese house without first removing your shoes, you will have broken one of their rules of good manners. The best way to act in foreign cultures is to watch other people and follow their example.

In North America, two famous books about manners, or etiquette, were written by Emily Post and Amy Vanderbilt. These books tell you things such as which fork to use at a dinner party or how to answer an invitation to a fancy ball. Sooner or later, someone else will write a book that will become the next guide to good manners. But if you're observant and considerate to others, you really won't need to buy the book!

What purpose did the first buttons serve?

It's hard to imagine getting dressed without doing up some buttons. But in ancient times, strings, pins and belts—not buttons—were used to fasten clothes together. The first buttons were used as jewelry!

Archaeologists have dug up ornamental buttons in Southern Asia that date from 2000 B.C. They were made by carving sea shells into circles and triangles, and piercing them with holes for sewing on clothing.

The early Greeks and Romans used shell buttons to decorate tunics and togas. They even attached wooden buttons to pins and made brooches. Finely carved ivory and bone buttons, covered with gold or studded with jewels, were found in European ruins.

Only in the 1200s, in Western Europe, did tailors think of making buttonholes across from the button so they could fasten a garment together.

DID YOU KNOW . . . legend says that in the 1500s, buttons were added to men's coat cuffs to prevent them from wiping their mouths on their sleeves! However, they were more likely used to close slits in sleeves.

What were the first shoes like?

The oldest shoe in existence is something we still wear today— sandals. Sandals, made of woven papyrus, or plant fibers, were discovered in an Egyptian tomb dating from 2000 B.C.

Sandals were the main footwear of peoples who lived long ago in warm climates. Ancient Greeks wore sandals made of leather which was dyed, decorated and gilded. The Roman sandal had a thicker sole, leather sides and was laced across the instep. The Gauls, (ancient French) preferred a high-backed sandal, while Arabs used a rope sandal of hemp and esparto grass.

The first recorded non-sandal shoe was a leather wraparound, shaped like a moccasin. Rawhide lacing tightened it against the foot. This was a favorite in Babylonia in 1600 B.C.

What becomes of old money?

At some time everyone has had worn out paper money in their purse or wallet. Or dollar bills patched together with tape. Usually we try to pass them on as quickly as possible before they fall apart. The life of bills is very short—especially the smaller denominations.

A one dollar bill is passed from hand to hand about 500 times before it wears out—usually within little more than a year. A five dollar bill is used only about 300 times and lasts about two years. The 20 dollar bill is passed 400 times and stays in circulation for five years.

So what happens to old money? It goes up in smoke. Banks ship the old bills back to the printing plant, where they are inspected by electronic equipment and human eyes to make sure that they aren't reusable or fakes. The bills are counted, canceled, bundled up and shredded. Then they are thrown into a special furnace and burnt. People called custodians watch the money burn to ensure that every note is completely destroyed.

How does the lead get into the pencil?

It may surprise you to discover that lead pencils aren't made out of lead! The writing material in a pencil is a mixture of graphite and clay.

The graphite and clay are blended with water in a powerful mixing machine. The mixture is then put into a machine that squeezes it out through a narrow opening. It comes out in the shape of a long string that is then cut into pieces, hardened in an oven and treated with wax to make it write smoothly.

The wood around a pencil is usually cedar because it has a soft grain and won't split when it is sharpened. The cedar is cut into narrow strips called slats. A groove is cut into each slat and a graphite string is laid in the groove. Then another slat is glued on top of the one holding the graphite. The result is a long pencil hot dog! This is then sanded, painted and cut into regular size pencils.

How does air help you drink from a straw?

Air helps you drink from a straw because of something called air pressure. The whole earth is surrounded by a layer of air more than a dozen kilometres (8 miles) thick. The weight of all this air is called air pressure, and every square centimetre on the earth's surface has one kilogram of air pressing down on it (14.7 pounds on every square inch). A milkshake has this weight of air pushing down on it. When you drink it through a straw you are lowering the air pressure in the straw. This negative air pressure pulls the milkshake up into the straw (and into your mouth) at the same time that the normal air pressure is pushing down on the milkshake.

What makes a tea-kettle whistle?

If you blow across the mouth of a bottle at the right angle you can make it whistle. A tea-kettle can do this too if the steam leaves the kettle in a certain direction. But not all tea-kettles whistle. Those that do have a lid covering their spout. This lid has a small hole in it. When the water boils, the steam produced can only escape through this hole, and it makes a whistling sound. A kettle without this special lid has an open spout that lets the steam escape in all directions. These kettles can't whistle as they work!

How do thermos bottles keep things warm?

Thermos is the Latin word for "heat," but a thermos bottle can keep liquids cold or hot. Thermoses are also known as vacuum bottles. A vacuum is empty space which contains no air molecules. A vacuum will not conduct heat so you can put a liquid inside a thermos and it will stay at its original temperature for a long time.

The bottle inside a thermos is made of two layers of silver glass. All the air between these glass walls has been pumped out. The heat is trapped inside the thermos bottle with nowhere to go.

Index _____